A NOTE TO PARENTS

When your children are ready to "step into reading," giving them the right books—and lots of them—is as crucial as giving them the right food to eat. **Step into Reading Books** present exciting stories and information reinforced with lively, colorful illustrations that make learning to read fun, satisfying, and worthwhile. They are priced so that acquiring an entire library of them is affordable. And they are beginning readers with an important difference—they're written on four levels.

Step 1 Books, with their very large type and extremely simple vocabulary, have been created for the very youngest readers. **Step 2 Books** are both longer and slightly more difficult. **Step 3 Books,** written to mid-second-grade reading levels, are for the child who has acquired even greater reading skills. **Step 4 Books** offer exciting nonfiction for the increasingly proficient reader.

Children develop at different ages. **Step into Reading Books,** with their four levels of reading, are designed to help children become good—and interested—readers *faster*. The grade levels assigned to the four steps—preschool through grade 1 for Step 1, grades 1 through 3 for Step 2, grades 2 and 3 for Step 3, and grades 2 through 4 for Step 4—are intended only as guides. Some children move through all four steps very rapidly; others climb the steps over a period of several years. These books will help your child "step into reading" in style!

Library of Congress Cataloging in Publication Data: King, P. E. (Patrick E.) Down on the funny farm. (Step into Reading. A Step 2 book) SUMMARY: A farmer thinks he is getting a bargain when he buys a farm for one dollar, until he finds that all the animals are mixed up about what they are supposed to do. [1. Farms–Fiction. 2. Domestic animals–Fiction] I. Graham, Alastair, ill. II. Title. III. Series: Step into reading. Step 2 book. PZ7.K58770n 1986 [E] 85-11893 ISBN: 0-394-87460-9 (trade); 0-394-97460-3 (lib. bdg.)

Manufactured in the United States of America   20

STEP INTO READING is a trademark of Random House, Inc.

Step into Reading

Down on the Funny Farm

by P. E. King
illustrated by Alastair Graham

A Step 2 Book

Random House New York

Once there was a farmer,

but he did not have a farm.

So one fine day

he set off to find one.

Soon the farmer

met an old man.

The old man was hard at work.

"Hello," said the farmer.

"What are you doing

this fine day?"

"I am pitching hay,"

said the old man.

"But where is your pitchfork?"

asked the farmer.

The old man held up

a table fork.

"Isn't it hard to pitch hay
with that little fork?"
asked the farmer.

"Yes," said the old man.
"It is very hard.
I am old and tired.
I do not want to work
on my farm anymore.
Do you know anyone
who wants to buy a farm?"
asked the old man.

"I sure do!"
cried the farmer.
"A farm is just
what I am looking for.
How much does your farm cost?"

"Two dollars,"
said the old man.
"Two dollars!
Are you crazy?"
said the farmer.

"Well, if two dollars
is too much,
then how about
one dollar?"
asked the old man.

"After all, my farm has

a horse,

a rooster,

a dog,

a chicken,

a pig,

and a cat."

"Sold!"

cried the farmer.

He gave the old man

one dollar.

The farmer was so happy.

"What good luck

that I met you!"

he said.

The old man was happy too.

He threw his fork away

and danced down the road.

Then the farmer went

to see his new farm.

A farm wagon stood

in the barn door.

"That is just what I need

to carry the hay,"

said the farmer.

Just then he heard

a soft noise—

"Whinny, whinny."

"That must be the horse,"

said the farmer.

"I will hitch it

to the wagon."

He went into the barn.

He did not see a horse.

But he did see a cat.

It was hitched

to the wagon!

The cat pulled and pulled.

But the wagon did not move.

"Whinny, whinny, whinny!"

said the cat.

The farmer laughed.

"You are not a horse!

You are a cat!

What are you doing

hitched to a wagon?"

asked the farmer.

"Whinny, whinny, whinny!"

answered the cat.

The farmer went outside

to find the horse.

Then he heard another noise.

"Cock-a-doodle-doo!"

The farmer looked up.

And what did he see?

A horse!

The horse was

on the barn roof!

"Cock-a-doodle-doo!"

crowed the horse.

"What in the world
are you doing up there?"
cried the farmer.
"You are not a rooster!
You are a horse!"

19

"There is something funny

about this farm,"

said the farmer.

He set off

to find the rooster.

Behind the barn

was a garden.

There was the rooster.

The rooster was busy

burying a bone.

20

"Woof, woof, woof!"

barked the rooster.

"No, no, no!" said the farmer.

"You are not a dog!

You are a rooster!"

Then the farmer set off

to find the dog.

He found the dog

in the henhouse.

The dog was sitting

on a nest of eggs.

"Cluck, cluck, cluck!"

said the dog.

"No, no, no!" cried the farmer.

"You are not a chicken!

You are a dog!

Now, where on earth

can the chicken be?"

He did not have to look far.
The chicken was in
the pigpen.
It was rolling around
in the mud!

"Oink, oink, oink!"

squealed the muddy chicken.

"You dumb cluck!

You are not a pig!

You are a chicken!"

said the farmer.

The farmer looked and looked
for the pig.
And at last he found it—
in the farmhouse!
It was chasing a mouse
around the kitchen.
"Meow, meow, meow!"
said the pig.

"This is all wrong!"

cried the farmer.

"Pigs do not chase mice.

Cats do.

You are not a cat!

You are a pig!

What a funny farm—

and what funny animals!

I can see I have a lot

of work to do."

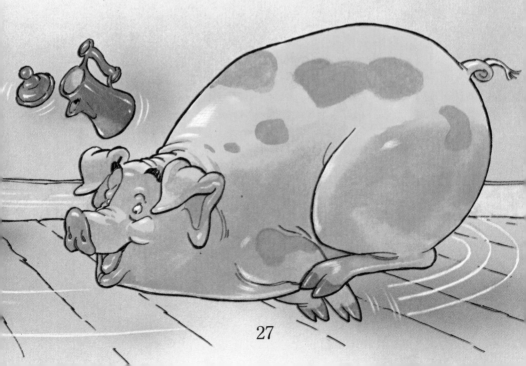

First the farmer took
the horse to the wagon.
He showed the horse
how to be a horse.
"Whinny, whinny, whinny!"
said the farmer.

"Whinny, whinny, whinny!"

said the horse.

"Very good!" said the farmer.

Next the farmer took

the rooster to the barn roof.

He showed the rooster

how to be a rooster.

The farmer threw back his head.

"Cock-a-doodle-doo!"

crowed the farmer.

"Cock-a-doodle-doo!"

crowed the rooster.

"That's right!" said the farmer.

Then the farmer took

the dog to the garden.

He showed the dog

how to be a dog.

The farmer dug a big hole.

He dropped a bone

into the hole.

"Woof, woof, woof!"

barked the farmer.

"Woof, woof, woof!"

barked the dog.

"Good boy!" said the farmer.

Then the farmer

showed the chicken

how to be a chicken.

And the pig

how to be a pig.

And the cat

how to be a cat.

At last each animal was in
the right place.
Each animal was doing
the right thing.
The farmer was happy.

The next day the farmer

went to work in his fields.

"I am lucky," he said,

"because I have a farm.

But I am lonely

because I do not

have a wife."

At that very moment

a lady came riding by.

"Did I hear you say

that you want a wife?"

asked the lady.

"I am looking
for a husband.
Your farm looks nice.
You look nice too.
I will marry you,"
said the lady.

So the farmer and the lady
got married.

The next day the lady said

to the farmer,

"I have a father.

He has no place to live.

Can he stay with us

on our farm?"

The farmer answered,

"Why, yes, of course!"

As soon as the farmer

said this,

the old man jumped out.

When the lady saw the old man,

she said, "Dad!"

When the cat saw the old man,

it went to the wagon

and said, "Whinny, whinny, whinny!"

When the horse saw the old man,

it climbed to the barn roof

and crowed, "Cock-a-doodle-doo!"

The rooster ran to the garden

with a bone and barked,

"Woof, woof, woof!"

The dog sat on the eggs

and said, "Cluck, cluck, cluck!"

The chicken jumped into the mud
and squealed, "Oink, oink, oink!"

And the pig ran to the mouse hole
and purred, "Meow, meow, meow!"

The old man put his arms around
his daughter and his new son.
"We are going to be
so happy together!"
he said.

Do YOU think they lived
happily ever after?